Acknowledgements

No man is an island. A thank you to those who helped and supported me on my journey so far.

Paul Taylor, Verity Lockhart, Ian Cheesman (and all those on E section back in the day), Dave Shepherd, James Asser, Justina Beekin, Howard Hodges, Barry White, Lou Hill, George Harrington, Lee Simmonds (and all those on A section back in the day), Mick Jones, Ian Still, Steve Warner, Bill Warner, Steve Tattersall, Steve French, Helen Campbell, Brad Lozynski, Ed Downs, Chris Bishop, Naj Al-Mussawi, Jo Munday, Martin Roberts (who started me off on this journey – Martin, it's your fault!), Rich McKenzie, Dave Hull, Richard Warr, Andy Haslem, Paul Constable, Jak Bower, Rob Walker, Jon Winter, Steve Rigby, Denis Sazonov, Dan Salter, Liam Tinkl. There are others. You know who you are.

Matt Pead, Alex Weir, Ethan Caines, Steve Snaith, Dave Morris, Chris Flynn, Tomasz Wojcek, Marcin Tominek, Jason Colgate, Rochelle Atwall, Ahnaf Choudhury, Neil Chisholm, Harry Keating, Dan Agostini, who have taught me comradery amongst colleagues exists outside of the police.

John Meakin & Ambika Kanungo, who believed in me, invested in me, and demonstrated the importance working for a good boss.

Most importantly, Mum, Dad, Beccy, Cheryl, Sophie, Julia, Leo, Josh and all extended members of my family. They have shown time and time again that love and loyalty can transcend seemingly any challenge.

Forward by the author

Timeline of events

I joined Sussex Police on 24th January 2004 as a Constable. After passing initial training and my probation, I joined then named West Downs division in a uniformed Neighbourhood Policing Team, stationed in Shoreham, West Sussex. Hand on heart, on my best day I was an average uniformed officer. I was lucky enough to serve alongside and learn from far more experienced officers, and I was always looking to develop myself.

In 2008, having passed PIP L2 exam, I joined Brighton & Hove division as a Trainee Detective Constable, and became a substantive Detective in 2009. I threw myself into this and loved being a Detective. In 2011 I passed Osprey Sergeants exam. After a couple of attempts at acting I could see I had a long wait before I would pass the board and be eligible for promotion. I attempted more specialised units but struggled to get released from the main office. I saw a growing trend in crimes where a significant element involved technology. Already confident in using IT, and in an effort to give myself a distinguishing edge from my peers, I self-funded my way through some basic IT and IT security qualifications. This introduced me to the world of cyber security, and I became fascinated. In 2014, Surrey & Sussex Police started the collaborated Cyber Crime Unit. I applied and was lucky enough to be successful.

In 2017, significant changes in my personal life meant I needed to drastically increase my earning capacity or face certain financial ruin. Whilst I had kept an open mind towards a career outside of the police, one day, necessity became the mother of invention. On 29th December 2017, I left Sussex Police, whilst not suspended or under any form of investigation.

As a warranted Officer, I served the Crown and protected and served the public without fear or favour. Now, as an Information Security Professional I help companies protect themselves and their customers from computer hackers, information thieves and cyber criminals. I also make it easier for employees to do the right thing, and harder to do the wrong thing. That is my business... and business is good.

Why this book?

In a word, loyalty. Loyalty to those whom I served, and those whom I had not the time or the opportunity to serve with. Loyalty to those who gave it their all but who burnt out, or wanted out and could not find a way. Loyalty to those who continue to serve, doing their best but who want to move on to the next chapter of their career.

I do not want a mass exodus from the police.

I don't. Far from it. Nothing is perfect, but I am fiercely loyal to the police as an institution and to the brave Officers and civilians who serve. I want you to keep doing what you are doing and do it well. I reject any 'de-fund the police' narratives. Society should expect the best from our police, and only the best, most capable applicants from as wide a diversity of society should be selected to serve. I want Officers to be well paid, well trained, rested and present in the situation they find themselves, exercising good judgement and held accountable for their actions. I want them to be there because of their passion for doing so. I want them to serve despite their ability to get a job elsewhere.

If you are a serving Officer and you love what you do, I sincerely thank you. Please keep doing what you do. This book is not for you.

This book is for the Officer approaching retirement or who is mid-career and looking to leave the police and pursue a career elsewhere, but whom is confused or daunted by the path ahead.

What qualifies me to write this book?

I enjoyed my police services and worked hard, but I do not consider myself to have been anything exceptional. Having decided that I needed to explore a career outside the police, I managed to formulate a plan to leave the job and after a couple of tries, successfully executed it. I am regularly contacted by serving Officers asking for advice and guidance on how to leave, trying to forge their own path.

This book builds upon conversations I have had with those who have contacted me for advice. It is my gift to other servicing Officers as an act of loyalty. I hope you find it useful. I'd love to hear from you if it is.

Contents

Introduction

Serving in the police is the best job in the world. The sense of purpose, the camaraderie, the adventure, the excitement. A chance to see the world through a different lens. Most importantly, the chance to serve and to make a difference. It was all these things for me, and I loved it. Over time though, what I needed changed.

There are thousands of interactions between the police and the public every day where the courage, sense of duty and compassion the police bring to the situation make a positive difference, and that opportunity to serve and to make the world a better place one interaction at a time is so rewarding.

I loved my time in the police. I am incredibly proud that I served. I would do it all again and I remain as 'pro' as you can get. But there came a time where it was no longer giving me what I needed. I flirted with the idea of leaving. I found resistance and scepticism when I discussed these thoughts with close colleagues, as though once in the police one could not do any other job. It was as though other jobs did not have the same importance or meaning, or that police skills were too unique to translate to another career. It was also as though no-other job within reach was as well paid or as secure as the Police.

I wrote this book out of loyalty to those colleagues who wanted to leave but could not find a path. I also want the best and the brightest in the police. It gave me a fantastic grounding, and propelled me forward in life, but it does not have to be a job-for-life.

Society benefits from having police officers who are there because they want to be, despite their ability to get a job elsewhere. Having people in the police because they believe they cannot do anything else serves no one; neither themselves nor (especially) the public.

If serving in the police is no longer working for you, you can leave. If the thought of doing so is daunting and the day-to-day pressures are consuming, it is all-to-easy to behave like a frog in a saucepan of water on the stove with the temperature slowly rising. Feeling trapped, scared to move, not noticing that you are slowly cooking in the environment around you.

If you love what you do, please keep doing that (and, maybe spend your time reading a different book?). We need people like you to continue serving the Crown and the public with bravery and compassion. If you are coming up to retirement or are currently serving and are considering leaving, I hope this book is of use to you. It lays out the path I took after many wrong turns, failed attempts and lessons learnt. Eventually I forged my own path, and if you are to leave you will have to forge your own. I hope some of the advice and anecdotes in this book helps you..

...In short, getting into the police may have been a long, hard, slow process.

Be prepared for leaving the police mid-career to be the same.

Making the decision to leave

"There is an unequal amount of good and bad in most things. The trick is to figure out the ratio and act accordingly." - TH3J35T3R

Many serving officers say they want to leave the police. They imagine. They toy with the idea. They look at the policing lifestyle, the shift work, the overtime, the job security, the fact their work is always going to be there. And whilst they may have lost the love for everyday police work, occasionally there is an absolutely blinding result where everything comes good, and they get some real justice for the victims. This makes the last three months or so of frustration worthwhile.

Perhaps you think to yourself *"Things have to get better soon. How long can it go on before they realise how bad things are and do something about it? Financially, I can cut back here and there. The Government has to ease up with the pay restrictions eventually, right?"*

If this describes you, I sympathise. I was there for a while too. You are not ready to leave.

After a while, either through burn out, frustration, financial pressure, internal politics, or the lack of career development and opportunities, you decide *"That's it.... I'm done. I want out.. I'll do it. I'll leave."*

You must get to the place where the risks associated with staying are worse than the risks associated with leaving. Only then will you commit to doing what is necessary to leave and stay the course when dealing with the rejection that is going to come with trying. Looking for a new job *is* (at least) a part-time job. To do all this extra work whilst you are serving, working the hours, dealing with the pressure that comes with the job – it is often just too tough to sustain the commitment past the first couple of rejections. You need sky high motivation and the discipline to grind on when it gets tough.

Find what motivates you

Joining the police can be a long winded and arduous process, yet you did it because the prize was worth the struggle. You were motivated enough to go through the recruitment journey and risk rejection.

Those who seek to leave the police have, by definition, different motivators. Mine was career progression and money. I became a father and I wanted to provide for my family. As I found when I eventually did leave, the world outside the police is not all milk and honey. I have bad days. I have boring days. At times I miss the police but I feel pride and gratitude that I held the badge and served the Crown, making a difference to people's lives. And now I am motivated to serve a new goal. My motivators are money, time and family. I strive for a balance between earning enough money to provide for my family, whilst getting enough time to spend with them in a job that also allows me to continue making the world a better place.

> *"He who has a why to live for can bear almost any how." — Friedrich Nietzsche.*

Why do you want to leave? Write your reasons down. They will be important when you come to target a future career.

Do you want to take control of your career? Do you need a job with less pressure? With less stress? Greater earning potential? A better work-life balance? Do you want to walk down the street and not be CRO spotting? Are you mentally and emotionally drained and need a different path? Do you want more control over your career?

To quote Mark Manson: *"Everybody wants what feels good. Everyone wants to live a carefree, happy and easy life, to fall in love and have amazing sex and relationships, to look perfect and make money, and be popular and well-respected and admired and a total baller to the point that people part like the Red Sea when you walk into the room.... A more interesting question—a question that perhaps you've never considered before—is what pain do you want in your life? What are you willing to struggle for? Because that seems to be a greater determinant of how our lives turn out".*

Trying to leave the police is going to take many hours of your time. It is probably going to require you to acquire new skills, to take yourself out of your comfort zone and to a place where people will probably reject you, and that hurts. It is going to take hours of work on your CV, on covering letters, emails, and job board postings. It is going to take hours of interview preparation, where your interview performance will incrementally improve but you will still not get offered a job, and that will disappoint. And when you are successful in the application process, you will have the choice to make; To feel the fear and leave the

fold – the certainty and security associated with the job
you know.

In short, getting into the police may have been a long, hard,
slow process. Be prepared for leaving the police mid-career to
be the same.

Job security.

I noticed a lot of people in the job saying words to the effect of
*". . . At least I 've got job security in the police. I can't be made
redundant"*. – I held on to that comfort for a long time until one
day I had an epiphany; job security does not matter. What
matters is employment security. Employment security allows
you to move roles and organisations in the same (or different)
sector. It spreads your risk. Employment security can be
measured as the time and effort it takes to move from one job
to another. The key to this is keeping in-demand skills up-to-
date and continuous learning. If you stay current in your chosen
field or study towards another field, and you have good
interpersonal skills, you need not fear losing your job. I know of
people who refresh their CV and have 'dry runs' at applying for
similar jobs to their own even when they do not want to change
jobs. If they get down to the final stages, they gracefully
withdraw knowing they are still current. If they struggle to get
interest, they know they need to rework their CV or add an
additional course or qualification to it. Do not seek job security
– it will leave you beholden to the success and the whims of an
individual organisation. Seek employment security. Trust in your
skills and your adaptability. You do not need to know the detail
of how. Come the moment, you will find a way.

Decision made: You are going to leave

You have made the decision to leave. You are daunted, but you are committed, and you ARE going to do it. How?

The Skill set of most police officers

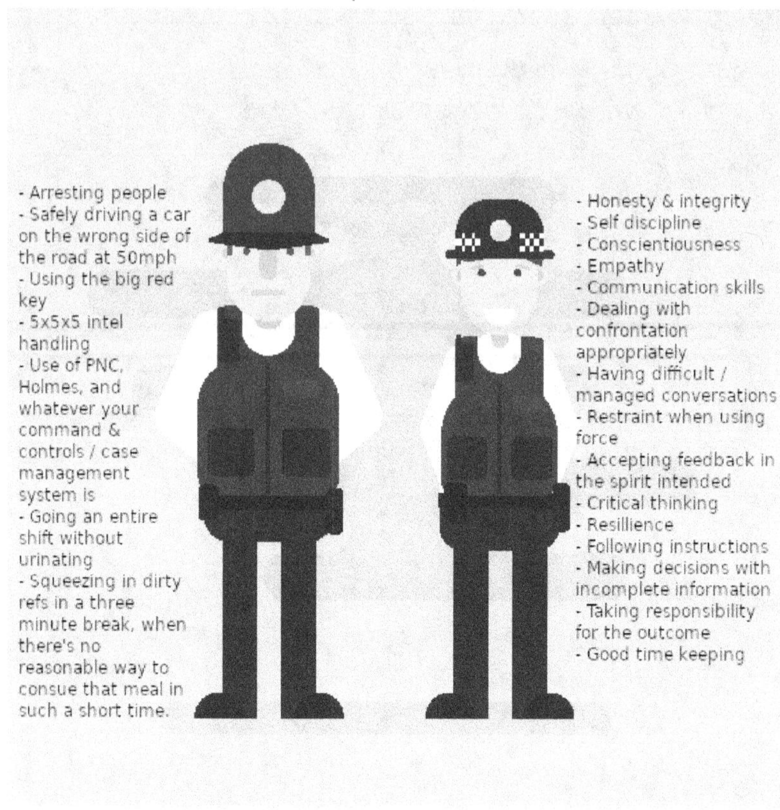

(Excuse my crappy diagram)

Transferable skills

The skills and experiences on the right are incredibly sought after in the outside world, and they are displayed by people who hold very senior positions. If these skills can be taught or trained, it takes a long time to do so. Private industry is crying out for people with these 'soft' skills, life experience and all-round competence. They are looking for people with these attributes. They are looking for someone like you, but they cannot hire you right away. Why not?

The CV is often where the early stages of job seeking effort is focused. Depending on experience before the police, most officers spend a lot of time detailing their skills and experience in ways only other police officers will understand or appreciate. This is understandable. How can you know what the 'real world' is looking for? Besides, you're a pretty good cop, right? They're going to be impressed with those skills, surely? And if not, you can explain what it all means in interview... right?

This next paragraph is the most important message of this book:

Having soft skills is not enough to get you a job with a comparable or even increase in salary. You must demonstrate how these skills are transferable to another industry. This is where most people trying to leave the police struggle. If you merely present yourself as an effective police officer in the hope that the hiring manager will see your potential in your policing skills and experience, you will struggle to make the transition. In my experience, it is rare to find a hiring manager to take you under their wing, give you a job and mould you into shape. If you have tried to leave the police but not been getting very far, this could be where you have been going wrong.

In my experience, this approach to job applications does not work and when it does, it is often for a role on the same or less money that you get in the police. If you are going to give up that job security and take on the risk of leaving what you know, you are going to want a pay rise now, or soon in the future to compensate you for taking that risk.

Organisations usually do not want to mould you into shape. As someone who has tried to hire someone into a team, I can attest to how hard and slow filling a vacancy is. You have work up to your eyeballs with your day job, not helped by the fact you have been carrying this vacancy for ages. Eventually leadership have approved the additional headcount, HR have done what they need to do to advertise the role and the applications come in. It takes ages to weed through them, and then there is the disappointment of interviews where your expectation of someone based on how they described themselves on their CV just does not match up with the person you meet in interview. You finally find someone. You offer the job. They accept, but they have a three-month notice period. You wait, only for them to pull out just before starting. Perhaps they got another offer or decided to stay in their existing role? It often takes 6-9 months or more to hire someone in, and by the time you do arrive, most hiring managers do not want to have to work too hard to mould you. They understand you need to onboard and get you up to speed with their culture and practices, but they want someone who is going to deliver their business needs soon, preferably by hitting the ground running.

I, and others who have left 'successfully' have taken the soft skills and experience gained from the police and combined those skills with industry relevant experience and qualifications.

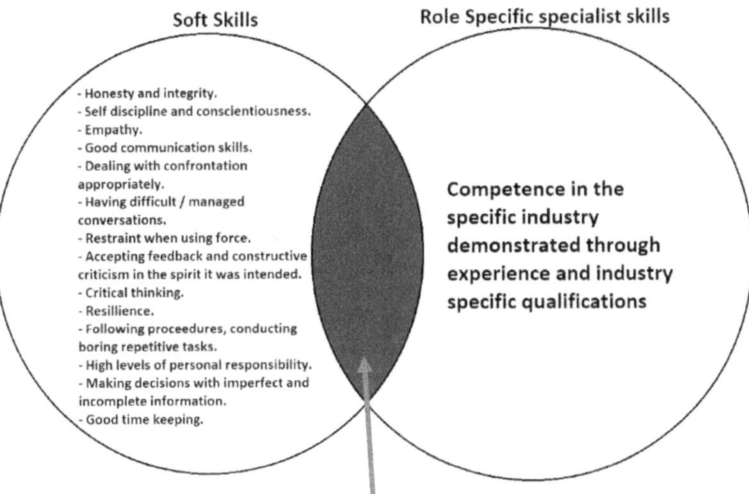

Your post-police career

Look at the figure above. The left circle, you should already have. So, what should you put in that second circle? What industry? What sort of role? This is for you to answer. Think back to the list you made of what motivates you. Then consider;

- What inspires you?
- What viable market is there for that skill set?
- What salary does it attract?
- What lifestyle would it give you?

Possible post-police careers

The following are some ideas of areas where there is achievable crossover with your police experience. There is a good chance you have done elements of this work in your police career already. It is not an exhaustive list. It is probably not a good list. I work in cyber security, so the other industries detailed below are not written from a point of experience or expertise. My gross over-simplification would probably offend practitioners. Have a read, and then start researching job roles in the industry below through the generic job boards (Monster, Indeed, Reed) to see what the demand for the job roles are in terms of numbers of positions and going salaries for someone established in that role and field.

Business Continuity and Disaster Recovery (BC/DR)

Business continuity is about having a plan to deal with difficult situations, so your organisation can continue to function with as little disruption as possible. Flood, fire, cyber-attack, supply change failure, losing a key employee, global pandemic, etc. Most of this is planning and table-top exercises and your attention to detail and practical, action orientated mindset will help you foresee issues and contingencies when planning for such emergencies.

If the bad thing really does happen, your experience responding to emergencies and dealing with a crisis with a calm, decisive manner will give you credibility. Your experience in operating in a Gold, Silver, Bronze chain-of-command scenario will give you gravitas.

Working out how a business can continue to function in a crisis and recover from a disaster is a large area of risk management. 'ISO22301' is the name of a standard of best practice you could research, as is 'NIST 800-34 Rev 1'. Numerous books exist that describe the process for planning for and running a business continuity / disaster recovery function about which, you can research best practice frameworks, and tools and increase your technical knowledge.

Physical security management

All businesses will be concerned about the security of their facilities and premises, their staff and their stakeholders. Some will be concerned enough to hire personnel to patrol and manage them. Some venues (entertainment venues) may have regulatory requirement to have staff. Read The Kerslake Report: An independent review into the preparedness for, and emergency response to, the Manchester Arena attack on 22nd. May 2017. It spells out the lessons learnt from this tragic event and gives a huge amount of detail into how physical security at large events should be done.

Governance Risk & Compliance

Governance in this context means the policy framework for how that business works. You have and follow force policies now. Every industry and organisation will have its own rules and policies for how it does what it does. Someone had to write those policies, and someone must review them regularly to make sure they are still fit for purpose.

Risk is identifying and managing risk (the private sector uses a different formula that is specific to their industry - but it is just a formula and framework. You learnt the National Decision-Making Model; you can learn the private sector models).

Compliance work can involve auditing (investigating) that you are doing what your policies say you should do. Auditing is a natural fit for ex-police who enjoyed investigation. You need to interview people, handle evidence (mostly documents), be good at report writing and have a sceptical mindset.

Project Management

A project is a temporary venture that exists to produce a defined outcome. It has agreed objectives as well as its own project plan, budget, timescale, deliverables, and tasks.

Do your reviews / write-ups at the beginning of an investigation cover the following:

What are we trying to do? When will we start? What do we need? Can we do it alone or do we need help from others? How long will it take? How much will it cost? (eg: Overtime? Staged forensic submission strategies). When you think about it, a complex investigation is a project. Project Management Professional, Prince 2 & Agile are all project management methodologies to research.

Recruitment

I know of officers who have used their people skills to become recruitment consultants – marrying up organisations with vacancies and candidates looking for roles. It will require your developed skills in patience, effective communication skills, and the ability to influence.

Safeguarding

Any organisation that deals with children, the elderly or the vulnerable will have concerns with safeguarding, school academies, local authorities, youth groups, hospitals, churches, care homes, charities. I know of multiple officers with safeguarding experience join sports clubs to head up their safeguarding roles.

Fraud investigation / prevention

An obvious fit for some, especially if you have some fraud investigation experience in the police. Perhaps you've got your Financial Investigation qualifications? If you have not, you probably need to study towards those.

This area of work can also involve some due diligence (research) into potential clients via Know Your Customer (KYC) and Anti-Money Laundering (AML) checks, making sure the client who wants to do business with you is not the direct relative of someone who is on the UN Sanctions List.

Trades

If you have, or can develop skills in a trade, this is a really good way to develop another career. I know of several officers who had awesome plumbing, kitchen / bathroom fitting, carpentry, and plastering skills from developing these skills at home after taking some leave and putting themselves through a small builders / tilers / plastering course and then were able to take on small jobs for good money.

I also know of ex-police who have started dog walking, child-minding, personal training, wedding and family / event photography, or domestic cleaning services. Going it alone as a sole trader can be a great idea if you have those skills. I know of people who reduced their hours to part time at the beginning and then submitting a business interest application, so they had some financial stability whilst building up a pipeline of work. Someone I know started a domestic cleaning company and drummed up business by standing outside a busy train station between 6am and 8am with a mop and ironing board handing out flyers. A lot of business came in from doing this over a couple of days.

You must be mindful that you will have used up your tax-free allowance in your police job, but remaining part-time keeps your pension topped up, and will give you no-end of clients. Coppers are always on the lookout for a trustworthy tradesperson. Be wary of 'mates rates'. The fact that you are trusted, honest and people can leave you to get on with it whilst they go to work should attract a premium, not a discount. Sure, you may have to do a couple of freebie jobs to get you started, but once you have those first couple of jobs under your belt, be wary about price being your differentiator from the competition. Do not try and be the cheapest. Someone will always do it cheaper. Be expensive but high quality. Six months in, you should be looking for at least 50% of the quotes you give to be turned down because you are too expensive. If everyone is saying 'yes' to you, your rates are too low.

Get some business insurance, a suitable vehicle (perhaps the one you have already got?), the minimum tools / equipment you need and a basic website and social media accounts so you can show off photos of your work (if appropriate), and you are away. Once you get some money coming in, consider an accountant – they will help you become efficient in taxes and expenses. Otherwise, do not forget to fill in your tax returns with HMRC every year!

Alan Miltz said "turnover is vanity, profit is sanity, cashflow is king". It does not matter how much money you are pulling in if all of it goes back out in expenses leaving you with no profit or nothing to pay yourself. Even if you are profitable, profitable businesses fail because of cash flow problems, not lack of profit. Having regular money coming in is vital. Think carefully about tying yourself in to monthly hire agreements of flash new vans or equipment you do not absolutely need before you have the pipeline of business and regular cash flow to sustain them.

Information security

This is the field I pursued. The salaries are good, the job openings are plentiful and the soft skills that you as a police officer have are highly sought after. Information security is different from IT. Information Security is taking a blend of risk, business knowledge and IT. There is lots of sub-fields you could specialise in and the technical skills required vary.

- Architecture (designing stuff) - very techie, requiring an all-rounder 'jack of all trades' level of Information Security knowledge.
- Engineering solutions (making it happen) - very techie – requires deep knowledge about how to implement and run specific solutions.
- Attack - very very techie, you must be able to program in at-least a scripting language.
- Defence - Quite techie.
- Governance / risk assurance / Auditing - a bit techie.

Architecture and engineering - These design a solution and then configure and operate it. Usually, people specialise in one specific technology. Cloud computing skills are incredibly sought after at the moment, and AWS and Azure fundamentals courses are often available for free.

Attack (red teaming, vulnerability testing) – This is hard, and requires solid tech skills. You need to be a command line hero, program in python, think in Linux, breathe Kali and be able to laugh at the futility of a Layer 4 firewall to protect the Active Directory server given your custom modified Proof of Concept exploit. If you know what I just said, and you have some demonstrable experience, good. Perhaps this is for you. If not, it is do-able but it is a long road of studying ahead. Check out attackdefense.com

Defence (incident response, cyber security analyst) - Tries to spot attacks and prevent them from happening or reducing the impact when they do. This lends itself well to the skills and experience gained in the police, providing you can evidence competence in digital forensics, WireShark, packet capture, Azure sentinel (although Microsoft will have changed the name of their Defence platform three times by the time you read this!) IDS / IPS / Snort / SecurityOnion / Elk Stack sort of tools and programs.

Governance, risk assurance / consulting, auditing has the least 'hard tech' skills requirements and the combination of people skills with a sceptical mind-set means this is the easiest transition to make.

IT sales

Police officers have good organisational skills and excellent communication skills, and most importantly will not come across as salespeople. This makes you ideal as someone to work in IT sales, provided you can onboard some technical skills.

I have an idea, now what?

Perhaps one of the suggestions above inspired you? Perhaps you already have your own idea. How do you go from idea to making it happen? Remember earlier I described the Venn diagram of your soft-skills and the industry specific skills required? This is how you start striving to fill in that circle on the right with role specific skills.

1) Download and read a report (eg: business continuity annual report)
2) Listen to podcasts on the subject
3) Register for webinars
4) Join a professional body as an associate member
5) Start studying for a qualification in that field
6) Find and connect with experts (LinkedIn is brilliant for this)

If you only take one thing away from this book, let it be this; *your soft skills gained in the police will get you 70% of the way to leaving, but that on its own is not enough. The last 30% required comes from you onboarding industry specific 'technical' skills, and (unless you are incredibly lucky) you get these from self-study. Choose something you are interested in and dig-in.*

Pitching yourself

The CV – half art, half science

The days of drafting your CV yourself before getting a mate to proofread it is over. In my opinion, it's something most police officers need expert help on. If you are a business that is advertising for a role, and you get 300 applicants (and they do), how on earth are you going to go through 300 different formatted CVs to decide who to interview? It is not humanly possible, so they use a computer to do it – they input some key terms into the programme and run the CVs against it. The 10 CV's that come out as the highest / closest match get put in front of a human, the other 290 get ditched. Your CV must first catch the eye of a computer, then catch the eye of a human. You can find pretty templates to use that make your CV look visually appealing, but I would not use them because the computer software has a hard time reading them, so you get screened out and your beautiful CV does not ever get seen by a human. Your CV needs to serve two audiences and a CV writing expert understands how this works and has their own copy of this software to see how yours stacks up. Expect to pay £100 - £500 for this service. I paid £300, but I got no-where in my applications with my CV before it went through a CV writing expert. Speculate to accumulate.

Because the CV experts need something to work on, you need to have a go at putting something together. Think of this stage as creating a 'stump CV' or rough template you will later tweak for specific roles. Work out what potential employers are looking for by looking at vacancies in the industry you are targeting; read job roles advertised and the lingo used in their industry press and social media feeds. Try to present your experience in the language and context of the industry you are targeting. Once you have written your stump CV find a service that boasts its ability to tailor to CV screening software, then begin on your covering letter.

The covering letter – allowing your personality to shine through

The covering letter expands on the information in your CV and allows you to express yourself more freely. You should use this letter to connect your CV to the job descriptions you are responding to. Draw up a template covering letter before getting a CV expert to review it. Remember, at the time a hiring manager reads this, they have a vacancy, and you are one of many potentials. They have the power and you do not. Your covering letter should convey a passion for the role and the industry and a belief that you are a good match.

Explain why you want to leave the police. "The job's f**ked and I want more money" is not a palatable reason even if it is partially true. Framing that sentiment as a desire for career development and new challenges is acceptable. There is a difference between the truth and complete transparency. Never ever lie on your CV or in an interview. Tell the truth but keep it in the context of the industry you are applying for. Talk about the cases you worked on where you had to demonstrate the skills of the chosen industry you are applying for.

TLA's

Avoid Three Letter Acronyms and police lingo at all costs. At the end of every line on your CV or covering letter, think 'so what?' - why would the person hiring you care? How does the skill or experience you are describing relate to the position you are applying for? Articulating your ability to arrest people, TPAC a car, buy drugs undercover, use a bespoke police computer system no-one outside of your world has heard of and submit swabs of body parts to a forensic lab will just drive a wedge between you the person looking to hire. Do not rely on them to work out its relevance or use to them. They won't. In-fact, they will worry that their job is more boring than yours and you will leave after a few weeks. Spell out why your skills are relevant to the role. It should be obvious to them having read your CV.

Money

Police pay scales are based on rank and service and the details are published online, so you have a pretty good idea as to what your colleagues earn. In my experience of the private sector however, no one talks about their own renumeration package, it is taboo, and most job offers describe their salary as 'competitive'. The only reason I can imagine is that there is quite a large variation, and I know from managing teams, people doing relatively equal work sometimes are paid very unequally. So how do you know what salary to ask for? Helpfully, in exchange for an email address and an agreement to receive marketing emails, some larger recruitment firms such as Robert Half publish regular salary guides that give you an indication of the going rate for salaries for different occupations. They will give you a ballpark, but they are only guides.

There is much more to a job offer than the headline salary (I will talk about this later) and all these should be factored in the round. When I have been recruiting for vacancies in my team, more than once, I've had my team re-set budgets to get a candidate who we really wanted but needed to significantly up the offer to meet their expectations. I have been able to negotiate a salary 45% higher than the original offer once I had convinced them I was who they wanted. Timing is key here; you cannot convince someone to open their wallet and stretch their budget until they have fallen in love with the idea of you coming on board. Use the salary guides as a ballpark to target roles that could give you the sort of salary you need. Let the process run its course and leave negotiations to the final stages of the recruitment process once offers are being made. Unless directly asked the question, my advice would be to avoid giving specific answers about money until you get down to final negotiations.

Back when I joined the police in 2004 we got two pay rises a year, the annual inflation alignment and you also got a rise as you gained another year in service or if you got promoted. This is quite different in the private sector. Most organisations will tell you that they conduct generous pay reviews annually. However, in my experience, once you are in role, pay reviews, if conducted at all, usually come up with the conclusion that you are at exactly the right salary, but may give you a small bonus. This means it is hard to progress up the pay scales once you are in a position, so negotiate hard at the beginning. I was once in a role where I discovered I was significantly below the market rate and tried over many months to get this reviewed. Despite appropriately pitched conversations with the right people, I was told absolutely nothing could be done, but 'don't worry' they said, – in six months' time it will be reviewed. Six months later when I raised the issue again, it was a further six months to wait. I could see the game we were playing; "Hold on today, there'll be jam tomorrow". So I found a job for the money I thought I was worth. When I handed in my notice a short while later, I was immediately asked to name what it would take to keep me, but I have a rule; never enter in to counter-offer negotiations once I've handed in my notice.

This is the lesson I learned; your salary is not based on how hard you work or how good you are at your job. It is a combination of three factors; how much value do you add, how easy are you to replace and the financial performance of the organisation (with vastly more emphasis placed on the second and third of these two factors).

Most employers will pay you not what you deliver, and not what you are worth, but what they think they can get away with paying. What I'm about to say is going to make me sound like the worst kind of narcissistic, self-aggrandising, grade A ass-hole, but hear me out. Out of us both, who adds more value to the world by showing up in their profession? You do. Who makes the world a better place? You do. Who gets paid more? I do. Why? There is a skills shortage in the cyber security world, I'm prepared to walk away and find another job, and there are less people out there that can replace me. Why is the Government so ready to suppress police salaries? They do not think vast numbers will leave (and I hope they are right), and even if they do, there is queue of fresh-faced hopefuls queuing out the door and around the block to join the police.

Social Media

Just like defence solicitors pre-trial, recruiters and hiring managers will research you. Lock down your social media. Delete controversial tweets, Instagram, Tik-Tok and public Facebook posts. You know the drill.

LinkedIn: It is mandatory. It is your 2nd CV. Everyone in the jobs market uses LinkedIn. Spend some time getting it right like your CV. If it is a clone of your CV, fair enough – it will help recruiters look for it, but you can add value if you comment on news items that are topical on the industry you are targeting. Avoid commenting on strictly police related news because you need to portray that you are not 'just' a police officer; you are a police officer who is ready to make a career transition to your new field. Beware allowing your snarky cynical side (a mandatory defence mechanism of cops) to shine through. I would frame every post you make as a positive.

The law of diminishing returns

By now you have put a lot of effort into leaving (well done) and it is natural to want feedback and even praise from those close to you. Everyone will have an opinion on your CV and covering letter, but not everyone's opinion should be weighed equally. If you show your CV to 10 people, you will get 10 different views and edit suggestions. You will know whose opinions you value most, but just be aware CVs and covering letters are half art and I would advise against endless tweaking based on yet another opinion. The true test will come when you start to apply.

Ready, aim, apply!

Once you have your new CV back from the CV writing specialists and the social media 'front of shop' is sorted, you are ready to start applying for jobs. Go back to those job sites you looked at before and upload your CV and covering letter. On your LinkedIn profile, flick the toggle over to 'open to work'. The user-interface keeps changing so if this is not immediately obvious, research how. This will allow recruiters and hiring managers within companies to find you based on key-word searches.

Actively target roles advertised on the job sites and LinkedIn. Also check out SecurityClearedJobs.com - they specifically target roles that require SC, DV and CTC clearance. (You'll know if you are SC or DV cleared, otherwise, as a police officer you will be CTC cleared). Most of these job search apps allow you to set alerts so you will get notified when new roles become available.

Looking for individual organisations hiring roles in your chosen industry is an obvious place to start. Also consider professional services firms. The big four, mid-tier, and boutique consultancy services need a constant flow of people coming into their business with specialist skills and experiences that can be sold on at a day rate to clients. Joining one of these firms gets you an impressive name on your CV and a wide exposure to lots of clients, which keeps you mentally agile. Sometimes this comes with travel, but in a post pandemic world most businesses encourage agile working.

When applying for roles, it is tempting to take the same CV and covering letter and spray them across multiple jobs that match what you are looking for. This technique will certainly get you through a volume of applications in a short amount of time. It is akin to swiping right on everything on Tinder; you are playing the numbers game. A hiring manager on the receiving end of this will have to work harder to pick out how your application matches what they are looking for, and when they have a volume of candidates, their first job is to weed out the ones who do not immediately and obviously match up.

If you have optimised your CV to a specific role that is the same in multiple organisations, this may work but you miss the opportunity to express yourself in your covering letter and convince the hiring manager why they should invite you for an interview. I recommend having a master copy of your CV and covering letter and save edited versions under a new folder for each role you apply for along with a copy of the job description (file, print, print to PDF). If you do not do this, many weeks later when you are invited for your interview, you may not be able to find the job description or what you wrote in your covering letter.

Your CV and covering letter should be tweaked slightly to optimise it specifically to that role, calling out specific requirements in the job description and how they align to your experience. This more targeted approach takes more time, so it is a trade-off, but remember it took you a long time to get into the police, so getting out is not a quick process and this bit can feel like a grind. Expect to apply to many jobs and never hear anything back. If you have applied for 50 jobs and not heard anything back, consider tweaking your CV or covering letter.

Be open to applying for jobs using a recruitment agent. Recruiters will know the industry, know what employers are looking for and will be able to translate your skills to the employers' requirements. A recruiter is looking to match candidates to vacancies, and as such they need a pool of candidates to draw upon, and they also need a pipeline of organisations looking to fill vacancies. They earn a percentage of your salary if they place you in an organisation successfully, but crucially you do not pay their commission – the organisation filling the vacancy does. If your salary is £50k and the recruiter charges the organisation 15%, then your job placement is worth £7,500 to the recruiter. This has the obvious effect of making you more expensive to the hiring manager compared with someone who has applied directly. It also makes good candidates valuable to recruiters, and they can sometimes tell you what you want to hear. In my experience, they can be very transactional in their nature – they call you up full of enthusiasm and you think they are really excited by your CV but then you never hear from them again. It is the nature of the market, I guess. There are recruiters who are willing to build relationships over the longer term and having that relationship with a recruiter who can act as a trusted advisor is worth its weight in gold. They will advise you on the process, provide feedback on your CV and can give you interview tips plus sample questions if you ask. They also act as a middle party and will lead on salary negotiations if you get this far. Their commission for placing you is usually based as a percentage of your salary, so the more you get paid, the higher their commission. However, they will tell you if you are being unrealistic in what you are asking for. Using LinkedIn to find industry specific recruiters is a good tip.

Understand that, given your background, in many cases you will be the wildcard candidate. You are, in effect, marmite. See this as a strength rather than a weakness. For better or worse, your prior experience will help you stand out. If you get an interview, it means you are off to a strong start. I have had plenty of interviews where, during the interview, the hiring manager has disclosed that either they or a close family member are or were 'job'. We still look out for each other after we hand in our warrant card.

Interviews (whilst not under caution)

Once you start getting interviews, you are in with a fighting chance. It is vindication that your covering letter and CV worked, or that the recruiter believes you have potential. Think of this as dating – it is a two way process. Everyone puts their best selves first and you need to look for a good match across a number of criteria.

What to expect

Expect there to be two or three stages of interview.

First stage interviews will probably be over video call. It could be with a member of HR who is looking to screen you off or pass you through to the next stage with the hiring manager or could be straight with the hiring manager. It is usually a walk through your CV to put a face to the document and let you tell your story about why you want to leave and how your experience relates to the role. There may be some competency questions, but cultural fit will be what is looked for; 'will this person fit in here?' is a key question they will be asking themselves.

If the first interview was with someone from HR, the second interview will often be with the hiring manager and your potential boss. If you spoke to the hiring manager in the first interview, the second interview will usually be with someone else on the team you are applying for. This is usually a bit more of a test of your subject matter knowledge but the 'culture and fit' is always being assessed so remain genial, upbeat and expect to give any new person you talk to a quick run through your CV and background.

If it goes to a third round, sometimes you are asked to do a presentation. Sometimes it is couched as an 'informal' chat with someone quite senior in the organisation to seal the deal. Do not expect structured questions here, more of a short summary of the company, the role and what they want you to help them accomplish.

The Seven P's of Preparation
This is how I prepare for an interview

- Set up a daily Google alert for the company.
- Read their website, especially their news.
- Most large organisations will espouse their culture and values publicly. Make sure you know these and be able to weave these values in your stories and examples.
- Look for them on the usual social media platforms. Read their last dozen or so postings.
- Search for the business on Companies House. Read the executive summary of their last posted accounts. If the company is in good financial health, great. If they are struggling think carefully and be sure to ask them about their financial stability.
- If they are a publicly listed company, search for them on MorningStar or some other financial website. If their share price has taken a large dip in the not-too-recent-past, investigate why and whether that bodes well for the future.
- If it is a large company, look to see who is on the Board of Directors or who is a Partner in an LLP
- Search for the business on GlassDoor – a website that allows employees to anonymously write about what it is like to work for their company. Expect to see highly polarised responses here. People who feel mediocre rarely post. It is often those who are angry and want to vent, or those who believe in their employer like a cult.
- Find out the names of those who are going to interview you and look them up on LinkedIn. If there are any

interests or commonalities, you can consider mentioning them in the interview.
- Re-read the job description and between the lines, bullet point examples of how you meet what they are looking for
- Have a coherent, positively spun answer to the following often asked questions:
    o Why do you want to leave your current role?
    o What are you looking for in your next role?
    o What is it about this role that made you want to apply?
    o What are your professional strengths?
    o What are your professional weaknesses?
    o Give an example of something you did that went badly wrong?
    o What do you do to develop yourself professionally?
- Make sure I have a list of questions to ask the interviewer(s) if given the opportunity.

Come the day, I show up slightly early, well groomed, wearing slightly more formal attire than the company dress code.

Frame every answer in a positive. There are lots of resources to help you prepare and career advisors or recruiters can help. If they ask, mention the ballpark salary you are looking for. A good stock answer is "Considering the role and the responsibilities you are looking the successful applicant to take on, I think somewhere between X & Y" and then stay quiet and try to read their reaction. Remember you are not at job offer yet.

Make sure you are prepared to ask two or three questions in every interview. There are plenty of resources out there that will guide you here. Be respectful of time limitations allocated for your interview. When I have interviewed for a position but have come to the end of the planned time in the schedule, I have stated "I've really enjoyed our chat and I have more questions to ask, if you'll permit me to ask them at a later stage or in another interview, I would really appreciate that".

Learn from the experience and enjoy

Once you get interviews, it's just a matter of time before you will get an offer. Keep going! Use the experience as practice. In the early stages, do not be afraid to take interviews for roles that are less than ideal. Better to learn, adapt and improve your technique for roles that are less-than your ideal job. Ideally you want to have a few good interviews under your belt before you apply for your ideal role. Remember, as a career changer, you're the wildcard candidate. Play that to your advantage. Depending on their existing team, an employer might appreciate the different experience and perspectives your soft skills bring in addition to your industry specific qualification and expertise.

Receiving job offers

Once you get a job offer verbally, they have shown their hand –
they want you. Now you are in a position of power to negotiate.
Think about all the elements of the offer. For example:

- Chemistry between you and your boss – is this someone
  you could get-on-with, and trust? (I've put this at the
  top of the list deliberately).
- Starting salary (remember, salaries seldom rise once
  you are in post, even if you are promoted).
- Bonus (how realistic is getting the bonus, i.e., how will
  they measure your performance to decide if you qualify
  for a bonus).
- Pension contributions (they are wildly different from
  industry to industry and from company to company.
  How much do you pay? how much do they pay?).
- Stock options?
- Private medical insurance, dental medical insurance?
- Holiday entitlement and buy-back options (buying extra
  days of holiday)
- Gym access

When an offer is made, negotiate specifics. Their offer is just
that, an offer. Ask them for more if you feel it is appropriate.

I tend to think of my career like a game of chess, or pool – if you
are doing it well you are planning two or three moves in
advance. Before I look to accept a role, I am already thinking
about the role after – will this role get me there? Will the boss
mentor and develop me in that direction? Will the name of the
company look good on the CV? Is the job title worded correctly?
I know of people who negotiate less on salary but on the
wording of their title and with good effect. They aimed to get
two years' experience in a role with a certain title so they would
be a contender for the next role up in another organisation. If

there is little wiggle room in the salary negotiations, but you like the role and the company and the boss, consider negotiating on the title. It will likely cost them little but could sling shot you on to the next move once you have done an acceptable amount of time in post.

Handing in your notice and leaving.

Until you get your new contract with the job offer in writing, do not do anything. Once you have it in writing, then you can consider handing in your notice. I have friends who have had offers made verbally and then rescinded a week or two later whilst they were considering the offer.

I've never been sky diving. It's not so much the fear of heights that has stopped me, it's the fear of falling. As I'm not talking from experience here, please indulge my imagination. I imagine being in the aeroplane climbing to jump altitude, the nerves and anticipation rising in my stomach. I imagine edging towards the exit, getting ready to make the exhilarating jump. After a "3, 2, 1" count down, I imagine sliding those last two or three inches and then tumbling into thin air; that last little shuffle forward being the result of a huge amount of purposeful action and training. The moment of exit would be a heroic act of bravery or certainty in one's capability and training. The first moments of free-fall, I imagine would be chaotic – spinning and acclimatising to the wind and the acceleration. Once settled into a free-fall position, I imagine the disbelief at the exhilarating and perhaps calm if noisy descent, without real knowledge of how far or fast you have come. Then the shoot opens, and your expectations must change as you begin the next stage of your descent.

Okay, I've tortured this metaphor enough now. Suffice to say it took a calculated risk and an amount of bravery to leave. I knew that provided I did not change my financial commitments and get used to a lifestyle on a higher salary, if leaving the police turned out to be a mistake, I could return within 5 years by doing a transferee's course.

The last day of my service was a massive round of "Thanks, good-byes and good-luck" (as well as a few investigation handovers – sorry about that). Handing over my warrant card and being escorted off the premises was just weird. The journey home knowing I had no powers felt weird. I wrestled with the loss of identity; If I was not a police officer, what was I?

The Change Curve

The first 6 months of leaving the police felt both like a whirlwind and some sort of weird holiday. Most of the time I felt out of my depth, out of place and a massive impostor. I wanted the safety and certainty of the police. Not-so deep-down, I still very much identified as a police officer.

The change curve is a well-documented phenomenon, and I've experienced it several times. Upon starting a new role, I have felt initial elation and sincere belief in the espoused values of the organisation, absorbing the culture and looking in awe at those around me at their confidence and competence. Each company has their own onboarding rituals and requirements, usually involving mandatory diversity and inclusion, health & safety, fraud & anti-money laundering training, as well as a load of policy documents for you to sign to say you acknowledge and will adhere to. Then there are the company values to learn and absorb. In his book 'Pour Your Heart Into It', Howard Schultz, CEO of Starbucks, spoke of corporate values;

"Experience has taught me that it's easy to talk about values, hard to implement them, and even harder for an outsider to

determine which values are heartfelt and which are window-dressing".

I think this is accurate. In the early stages of my time in an organisation, I have been guilty of wanting to not be a typical cynical copper, and proactively placing individuals (especially those in leadership positions around me) on pedestals and believing the values of the organisation to their purest interpretation. People are still people. Some are good. A few are great. Everyone is flawed. When you are in 'the job' you are paid to look for and predict the worse in people (and often are right, disappointingly). In my role in the corporate world, I've found more success by having a generous interpretation of people their actions and intentions.

After three months or so, the shine of a new organisation can wear off, as you get to know the corporate politics, who's who, their position, motivation and foibles. As different circumstances, difficulties and opportunities arise, you learn the "tight-loose" extent of the different corporate values, and how they are applied. For me, this is the danger period. This is the bottom of the change curve, where I know a bit about an organisation, but not yet enough to be truly effective. This is when I write an email to someone about an issue that is not in-line with someone else's' interpretation of the corporate values. Another challenge I have is to mix up people with very similar names within the same organisation. This acclimatising of corporate knowledge makes this the least enjoyable part of a transition or change. I've heard it said that it takes a year to get to know a role, and another year to refine and improve upon your performance in the role. After three years in a role, you have probably learnt around 80 – 90% of what there is to know, and if you wish to grow you should consider moving or growing your role. Once you've made the leap the initial leap, the following ones come easier.

(i) seek out a mentor – someone established and experienced in the field you are in and is willing to advise you – this person should preferably not be your line manager, although I have had boss' I trust implicitly enough to be a mentor.

(ii) Invest in and build your network. Get known amongst peers in your industry but not in your organisation. They will give you advice and guidance and open doors for you in the future.

You are the master of your own destiny. Your career is in your hands. Go forward.

www.ingramcontent.com/pod-product-compliance
Lightning Source LLC
Chambersburg PA
CBHW070059260726
48658CB00002B/914